THRIVE IN THE DISCOMFORT ZONE

Learn How To Do Things You Hate

BY

MATHEW C. WALTER

TABLE OF CONTENTS

FOREWARD ···- 4 -

CHAPTER ONE ··- 7 -

Setting Clear and Specific Goals ····································- 7 -

Understand the Power of Delayed Gratification ···········- 11 -

Cultivate Intrinsic Motivation ·····································- 15 -

Create a Detailed Plan ···- 19 -

CHAPTER TWO··- 23 -

Practice Self-Awareness ··- 23 -

Develop Self-Control ··- 26 -

Build Habits ··- 30 -

Embrace Discomfort ···- 34 -

CHAPTER THREE ···- 38 -

Develop Resilience ··- 38 -

Understand Resilience: ··- 38 -

Use Rewards and Punishments ·····································- 42 -

Seek Social Support···- 46 -

Monitor Progress··- 50 -

CHAPTER FOUR ··- 54 -

Visualize Success···- 54 -

Stay Consistent ··- 57 -

Practice Self-Compassion···- 61 -

Review and Reflect ···- 65 -

Patience and Persistence ··- 68 -

FOREWARD

Welcome to "Thriving in the Discomfort Zone," an extraordinary investigation of one of life's greatest paradoxes: the road to success frequently takes us through areas we'd rather avoid. You will set off on a life-changing adventure across the varied countries of sports, health, business, and education in the pages that follow. This journey is proof of the human spirit's unbreakable strength and the incredible ability for development that everyone of us possesses.

We are frequently told to follow our passions and look for comfort wherever we can in our pursuit of success. However, life has a way of presenting us with obstacles that force us to leave the comfortable boundaries of our comfort zones. We learn the most about ourselves when we are forced to complete tasks that we may loathe.

"Thriving in the Discomfort Zone" is a manual for people who are willing to accept discomfort as a means of achieving greatness. It is for those who are committed to improving their health, even when it means making sacrifices, such as athletes who understand that progress lies beyond their current limitations, business owners who understand that innovation thrives in uncertainty, and students who yearn for knowledge beyond their comfort zones.

You'll read about people in these pages who overcame hardship, faced their fears, and used discomfort's transforming ability to achieve extraordinary success.

You'll study practical techniques to take on the activities you may detest with a new-found sense of purpose as well as the psychology of perseverance and the science of resilience.

You'll learn from reading this book's chapters that discomfort is not a foe to be avoided but rather a steadfast companion on the road to greatness. It serves as the forging ground for our qualities, the engine for development, and the backdrop to our greatest triumphs.

"Thriving in the Discomfort Zone" is proof that the human spirit can adapt, change, and thrive despite hardship.

It serves as a reminder that success is not just for a select few people, but is instead within reach of anyone ready to take on the task, put up with the discomfort, and persevere with unyielding resolve.

I invite you to immerse yourself in the narratives, observations, and useful advice presented in these pages. As you travel the rocky terrain of your aspirations, let this book be your guide. May it give you the courage to take on the chores you detest, help you uncover your inner reserves of strength, and ultimately help you thrive in uncomfortable situations, paving the way for your success in business, sports, health, and education.

Your journey starts right here. Accept your discomfort. Accept the potential. Accept your potential. We're glad you're here at "Thriving in the Discomfort Zone."

"The future depends on what you do today."
- Mahatma Gandhi

CHAPTER ONE

You can accomplish everything you set your mind to. The idea that anything can be accomplished via self-control and accepting suffering is a potent one with roots in applied psychology. Understanding the fundamental ideas guiding motivation and behavior in people is necessary for this strategy.

Setting Clear and Specific Goals

Set specific goals for yourself first. Make sure they are SMART goals—specific, measurable, achievable, relevant, and time-bound. You are motivated and given direction when you have a defined goal.

A vital step in obtaining anything you desire is setting clear, defined goals, and applied psychological principles strongly support this. Goals that are clear and precise offer motivation, direction, and a framework for planning and measurement. Based on applied psychology, the following is a thorough description of how to set such goals:

Identify Your Desires and Values:

Determine your true desires and values in life to begin with. In order to feel intrinsically motivated and have a feeling of purpose, your goals should be in line with your basic values and desires.

Make Your Goals SMART:

The letters SMART, which stand for Specific, Measurable, Attainable, Relevant, and Time-bound, are an acronym. Let's examine each element in detail:

Specific: Your objective should be unambiguous and clearly stated. What, Why, and How questions ought to be addressed. It is simpler to work for a goal that is more definite.

Goals should be **Measurable** so you can keep track of your progress and know when you've reached them. Include specific metrics or measures of achievement.

Achievable: Confirm that your objective may realistically be attained in light of your present resources, abilities, and situation. Unattainable objectives can cause frustration and discouragement.

 Relevant: Your objective ought to be consistent with your larger objectives and values. It must be applicable to your life and make a significant contribution to your career or personal growth.

Time-bound: Establish a target date for completing your task. A deadline fosters a sense of urgency and discourages procrastination.

Use Positive Language:

Set up your objectives in a gratifying and encouraging way. Rather than stating, "I want to stop procrastinating," change your statement to, "I want to be more focused and productive." The language that is upbeat and empowering is more motivating.

Write Your Goals Down:

Describe your goals in writing. Writing them down makes them more real and strengthens your resolve to accomplish them. them. You can keep a journal or create a vision board to visualize your goals.

Prioritize Your Goals:

If you have several objectives, order them in order of importance and urgency. You can better allocate your time and energy as a result.

Visualize Your Success:

Use visualization tools to help you clearly picture reaching your objectives. This mental practice can boost motivation and help you form a distinct mental picture of success.

Develop an Action Plan:

Describe the precise processes and actions you must take to accomplish your objectives. A well-organized plan gives you a route to follow.

Set Performance Goals, Not Just Outcome Goals:

Performance objectives put the emphasis on the actions and behaviors necessary to attain the intended result, whereas outcome goals identify the desired result. For instance, you could create a performance objective to "exercise for 30 minutes every day" rather than "lose 20 pounds."

Track Your Progress:

Keep a close eye on your progress toward your objectives. Keep track of your successes, failures, and any changes you make to your strategy. Staying on track requires regular self-monitoring.

Seek Feedback and Adjust:

Don't be afraid to ask reliable friends, coaches, or mentors for their opinions. Your aims and tactics can be improved with the support of their opinions, which can offer insightful information.

Stay Committed and Adapt:

Being committed and being ready to adjust to new situations or potential barriers are essential for reaching your goals.

Celebrate Milestones:

Celebrate your accomplishments as you go along, especially as you hit certain milestones. This encouraging feedback will help you stay motivated and keep going.

Review and Reflect:

Periodically review your goals to ensure they remain relevant and meaningful. Reflect on your progress and adjust your goals or strategies as needed.

Stay Persistent:

Recognize that achieving worthwhile goals frequently calls for perseverance and endurance. Setbacks shouldn't demotivate you; instead, consider them an opportunity to improve.

Goal-setting that is based on applied psychology principles offers a strong foundation for both personal and professional development. You'll be more able to accomplish anything you want if you adhere to these instructions and stay dedicated to your objectives. Keep in mind that achieving achievement takes time, and an essential component of that trip is the process of establishing and pursuing certain goals.

Understand the Power of Delayed Gratification

Delaying short-term comforts or pleasures in favor of long-term benefits is a common need of self-control. The idea of delayed gratification is crucial for completing important objectives. Recognize that the suffering you feel now will eventually lead to greater satisfaction.

A key idea in applied psychology called the power of delayed gratification can greatly increase your capacity to attain your objectives and do anything you want. The capacity for delayed gratification is the ability to reject the lure of instant gratification in favor of bigger, longer-lasting rewards. How to use this power is explained in full here:

Recognize the Marshmallow Test:

The well-known Stanford Marshmallow Experiment in the 1960s helped to popularize the idea of delayed gratification. Children in this study were offered the option of one marshmallow now or two marshmallows later. The outcomes of their lives, such as academic performance and improved emotional control, were better in those who could wait for the bigger prize.

Understand the Brain's Reward System:

Understanding the brain's reward system is essential to understanding delayed gratification. When we receive immediate rewards, the brain produces dopamine, a chemical linked to pleasure. But the brain also has the ability to process delayed benefits, which encourages us to work toward goals by anticipating bigger rewards in the future.

Grasp the Importance of Impulse Control:

Impulse control, or the capacity to manage and control our immediate urges and impulses, is necessary for delayed satisfaction. It entails putting long-term objectives ahead of short-term urges.

Link it to Goal Setting:

Start by establishing precise, definite, and doable goals before attempting to use delayed gratification to your goals. Recognize that achieving these objectives frequently necessitates forgoing current pleasures in favor of higher long-term advantages.

Visualize Long-Term Rewards:

Make a clear mental picture of the long-term benefits and rewards you'll enjoy once you reach your objectives. Your motivation to put off gratification may increase if you can visualize these benefits.

Develop Self-Awareness:

Recognize the things that make you want fast gratification. Determine the circumstances, feelings, or settings that influence impulsive behavior. Your ability to address these triggers proactively is enhanced by self-awareness.

Practice Mindfulness:

Your ability to stay in the moment and control impulsive behavior can be enhanced by using mindfulness practices like meditation. You learn to examine your thoughts and feelings with no instant response through mindfulness.

Use Willpower Wisely:

A limited resource, willpower can run out over the day. Use it wisely by planning your day so that you can deal with difficult chores while your willpower is strongest, usually in the morning.

Employ Time Management Techniques:

You may prioritize long-term goals over momentary distractions with the help of effective time management. You can manage your time effectively by using tools like calendars, to-do lists, and goal-setting applications.

Create a Delayed Gratification Strategy:

Create a plan for dealing with temptations and quick rewards. This can entail physically removing distractions, establishing quick goals, or moderately rewarding yourself when you reach them.

Monitor Progress and Reflect:

Evaluate your development toward your long-term objectives frequently. Consider how your capacity to postpone gratification has helped you succeed. Celebrate your accomplishments as you go.

Practice Patience:

Recognize that patience is necessary for delayed gratification. On your trip, be ready for obstacles and hurdles. Keep going and keep your eyes on the prize at the end.

Learn from Failures:

Consider your cave-in to instant gratification as a learning opportunity rather than a setback. Develop ways to avoid the gap in the future by analyzing what caused it.

Seek Support and Accountability:

Share your objectives and dedication to delayed gratification with loved ones, close friends, or a mentor who may act as a sounding board and source of support.

Cultivate a Growth Mindset:

Adopt a growth mindset, which is the idea that with experience and effort, you can get better at delaying gratification and achieving long-term goals.
You may improve your self-control, make wiser decisions, and ultimately accomplish anything you want by realizing the importance of delayed gratification and incorporating these ideas into your life. It is a talent that may be developed over time and is essential to success in many facets of life.

Cultivate Intrinsic Motivation

The urge to achieve something for its own fulfillment rather than for the external rewards is known as intrinsic motivation. Your goals may contain intrinsic drive. Why is accomplishing this objective meaningful to you personally? Your self-discipline will be sustained by this inner desire.

A fundamental psychological idea that can assist you in achieving practically anything in life is cultivating intrinsic motivation. Intrinsic motivation is the internal drive and sincere desire that originate from inside as opposed to being influenced by rewards or pressures from without. Using the principles of applied psychology, the following is a thorough description of how to develop intrinsic motivation:

Understand Intrinsic Motivation:

Learn what intrinsic motivation is and why it's important for reaching your goals before you do anything else. Your individual interests, values, and sense of purpose are the foundation of intrinsic motivation. It's the pleasure and fulfillment you get from engaging in the activity.

Identify Your Values and Passions:

Think about your deepest beliefs and desires. What pursuits or hobbies fit these interests and values? Recognize that when you're doing something that aligns with your core values and passions, intrinsic motivation is frequently at its highest.

Set Meaningful Goals:

Make sure your objectives have relevance for you personally. Having a goal that is in line with your values and interests increases its inherent motivation. Think about your priorities and make goals that are consistent with them.

Find Autonomy and Control:

Intangible motivation is significantly influenced by autonomy. Look for chances where you may decide what to do and how to do it. Your intrinsic drive is increased because you feel in control of your fate, which boosts your sense of autonomy.

Set Clear and Challenging Goals:

When you're working on things that are neither overly simple nor overly complicated, your intrinsic drive is likely to be at its highest. Set hard but attainable goals since they will motivate you and increase your drive.

Focus on Mastery and Learning:

Develop a growth mentality, which places a strong emphasis on learning and development. Consider your objectives as chances for skill and personal development. This emphasis on mastery has the potential to boost intrinsic drive.

Connect to Your Sense of Purpose:

Think about how your objectives fit into a larger feeling of fulfillment or purpose. You're more likely to feel intrinsically driven when you can see the wider picture and realize the influence your work has.

Find Inherent Enjoyment:

Find the parts of your objectives or duties that you actually like doing. Finding the enjoyment that comes naturally from doing what you do can be a great source of intrinsic drive.

Set Intrinsic Rewards:

Create intrinsic benefits for yourself rather than relying entirely on rewards from the outside world. Personal fulfillment, a feeling of success, or the delight of artistic expression are a few examples.

Foster Curiosity and Interest:

Goal-setting should be done with an open mind and curiosity. Develop a sense of wonder and fascination, since this can inspire a desire to learn more and explore new things.

Overcome Challenges and Obstacles:

Recognize that obstacles and failures are a normal part of the path. Accept them as chances for development and education.

Overcoming challenges can make you more intrinsically motivated as you develop your abilities and resilience.

Stay Mindful and Present:

To remain focused and present in your duties, practice mindfulness. Because you're focused on the task at hand while you're fully present, you're more likely to feel intrinsically motivated.

Seek Intrinsic Feedback:

Be mindful of your internal feedback mechanism. While pursuing your objectives, pay attention to your feelings. Your intrinsic motivation is in action if you experience happiness, curiosity, or fulfillment.

Surround Yourself with Support:

Find a friendly setting where you may discuss your interests and aspirations with people who share them. By offering support and a sense of belonging, social support can strengthen your intrinsic motivation.

Reflect and Adjust:

Consider your progress frequently and revise your objectives or tactics as necessary. It's crucial to keep in line with your changing ideals and passions because as you change, your core drives could also change.

Applying these applied psychology principles and concentrating on intrinsic motivation will help you create a strong internal drive that will help you go forward with your goals. You'll find the will to persevere and succeed in almost any effort when you sincerely appreciate what you're doing and have a strong sense of purpose.

Create a Detailed Plan

Divide your objectives into more achievable, smaller activities. Create a detailed plan that specifies what must be done and when. This lessens emotions of overwhelm and provides you with a path to take.

Making a thorough strategy is an essential first step in reaching any objective, and it is firmly based on the principles of applied psychology. Here is a thorough explanation of how to build a thorough plan based on these guidelines:

Define Your Goal:

Start by outlining your objective in detail. Make it SMART, which stands for Specific, Measurable, Achievable, Relevant, and Time-bound. This makes sure that your objective is clear and simple to pursue.

Break Down Your Goal:

Your main aim should be broken down into smaller, more doable milestones. The road to achievement becomes more manageable and less intimidating when it is broken down.

Prioritize Your Sub-Goals:

Not every sub-goal is equally significant. Put them in order of importance and contribution to attaining the ultimate objective. Determine which sub-goals are necessary to achieve the others.

Set Deadlines:

Give each milestone and sub-goal a precise due date. Setting deadlines in advance gives you a sense of urgency and keeps you on course.

Identify Resources:

Establish the resources you'll need for each sub-goal. Time, money, expertise, skills, and assistance from others are all examples of resources.

Develop Action Steps:

Outline the precise steps you must take to accomplish each sub-goal. Be specific and in-depth. How, when, where, and what measures will you take to complete these tasks?

Consider Potential Obstacles:

Be prepared for any difficulties and hurdles that can appear on your route. Both internal and external limitations, such as a lack of enthusiasm or time constraints, may be present. Create plans to get around these challenges.

Use Implementation Intentions:

Specifying when, when, and how you plan to take action to accomplish your goals is known as setting implementation intentions. According to research in applied psychology, using this strategy can improve your chances of completing your plan.

Create a Schedule:

Make time in your daily, weekly, or monthly calendar to work on your sub-goals. Regard the time required for each work honestly.

Monitor Progress:

Create a mechanism for monitoring your advancement. Depending on the situation, this can entail making a checklist, using a project management app, or just keeping a journal. Review your progress frequently in relation to your plan.

Seek Accountability:

Tell a mentor, family member, or trusted friend about your goal so they can help hold you accountable. Checking in with someone who supports your goals on a regular basis can help you stay motivated.

Adjust and Adapt:

Be adaptable and receptive to changes. Because of how unpredictable life is, everything could change. Change your plan if unanticipated difficulties or opportunities arise.

Visualize Success:

Visualize a positive outcome. Think on accomplishing your objectives. Your motivation and confidence can both be increased by this mental practice.

Stay Focused:

Think of a successful result. Keep your goals in mind as you work. This mental exercise might help you become more motivated and self-assured.

Reflect and Learn:

Consider your development and experiences on a regular basis. Refine your strategy and approach by drawing lessons from your triumphs and mistakes.

CHAPTER TWO

Practice Self-Awareness

Understand your strengths and weaknesses, as well as the situations that trigger procrastination or discomfort. Self-awareness helps you identify potential obstacles and develop strategies to overcome them.

Practicing self-awareness is a fundamental aspect of achieving your goals based on applied psychology. Self-awareness involves understanding your thoughts, emotions, behaviors, strengths, and weaknesses. It enables you to make more informed decisions, manage your actions, and align them with your goals.

Mindfulness Meditation:

Mindfulness meditation is a practice that involves paying attention to the present moment without judgment. It helps you become more aware of your thoughts and emotions. Set aside time each day for mindfulness meditation to observe your inner experiences.

Journaling:

Keep a journal where you record your thoughts, emotions, and daily experiences. Reviewing your journal entries over time can reveal patterns in your thinking and emotional responses, enhancing self-awareness.

Self-Reflection:

Regularly set aside time for self-reflection. Ask yourself questions like, "What am I feeling right now? Why am I feeling this way?"

This introspective process helps you understand your emotional reactions and thought patterns.

Seek Feedback:

Ask for honest feedback from trusted friends, family members, or mentors. Others may notice things about you that you're not aware of. Be open to constructive criticism and use it as an opportunity for self-improvement.

Assess Your Strengths and Weaknesses:

Identify your strengths and weaknesses objectively. Consider using tools like personality assessments or 360-degree feedback to gain a better understanding of your qualities.

Set Goals and Priorities:

Self-awareness can help you clarify your values and priorities. Set specific goals that align with your values and reflect on how your actions contribute to these goals.

Monitor Your Thoughts:

Pay attention to your inner dialogue. Are you frequently self-critical or negative? Challenge and re-frame negative thoughts into more positive and constructive ones.

Identify Emotional Triggers:

Recognize the situations or events that trigger specific emotional responses. Understanding your emotional triggers can help you manage your reactions and make more rational decisions.

Practice Emotional Regulation:

Learn techniques for regulating your emotions, such as deep breathing, mindfulness exercises, or progressive muscle relaxation. These practices can help you stay calm and focused, even in challenging situations.

Seek Professional Help:

If you have difficulty accessing your emotions or addressing deep-seated issues, consider working with a therapist or counselor who specializes in self-awareness and personal development.

Assess Your Core Beliefs:

Examine your core beliefs and values. Are they helping or hindering your progress? Adjust your beliefs to better align with your goals and values.

Embrace Vulnerability:

Allow yourself to be vulnerable and open to personal growth. It's okay to admit your mistakes and limitations. Vulnerability can lead to greater self-awareness and resilience.

Create a Feedback Loop:

Continuously assess your progress. Regularly review your goals, actions, and the results you're achieving. Adjust your strategies as needed to stay on track.

Surround Yourself with a Supportive Network:

Build a network of people who support your personal growth and self-awareness journey. Engage in open and honest conversations with them to gain different perspectives.

Practice Self-Compassion:

Be kind and compassionate toward yourself as you explore your inner world. Self-compassion allows you to accept your flaws and imperfections while still striving for self-improvement.

Practicing self-awareness is an ongoing process that can lead to greater self-understanding and personal growth. By becoming more in tune with your thoughts, emotions, and behaviors, you can make conscious choices that align with your goals, ultimately increasing your chances of achieving anything you set your mind to.

Develop Self-Control

Self-control is the ability to resist immediate temptations in favor of long-term goals. Train yourself to make conscious choices that align with your objectives. Techniques like mindfulness meditation can help improve self-control.

Developing self-control is a critical skill when it comes to achieving your goals, and it's deeply rooted in applied psychology. Self-control enables you to resist immediate temptations and stay focused on long-term objectives. Here's a detailed explanation of how to develop self-control to achieve anything you want, drawing from applied psychology principles:

Understand the Importance of Self-Control:

Start by recognizing why self-control is crucial for success. Understand that it allows you to make better decisions, avoid impulsive choices, and stay committed to your goals even when faced with distractions or discomfort.

Increase Self-Awareness:

Self-awareness is a fundamental aspect of self-control. Understand your triggers for impulsive behavior and recognize the situations or emotions that lead you to lose control. This awareness will help you anticipate and manage these triggers.

Practice Mindfulness Meditation:

Mindfulness meditation can enhance self-control by improving your ability to focus on the present moment and manage impulses. Regular practice can increase your self-awareness and emotional regulation.

Use Cognitive Strategies:

Cognitive strategies involve changing your thought patterns to improve self-control. For example, you can re-frame temptations as potential obstacles to your goals and remind yourself of the long-term benefits of self-control.

Create a Structured Environment:

Modify your environment to reduce temptations and make it easier to exercise self-control. For instance, if you're trying to eat healthier, keep unhealthy snacks out of your home.

Set Clear Boundaries:

Establish clear boundaries and rules for yourself. These rules serve as guidelines that reinforce self-control. For example, setting a rule to work on your project for a certain amount of time each day.

Develop Healthy Habits:

Habits can automate behaviors, reducing the need for conscious self-control. Cultivate positive habits that align with your goals, and they will become second nature over time.

Use Willpower Wisely:

Willpower is a limited resource that can be depleted. Use it strategically by prioritizing important tasks early in the day and minimizing decisions on less critical matters.

Practice Delayed Gratification:

Delayed gratification is the ability to resist immediate rewards for larger, long-term gains. Practice this skill by intentionally delaying small pleasures and focusing on the bigger picture.

Visualize Success:

Visualization techniques can help you mentally rehearse self-control in challenging situations. Imagine yourself making disciplined choices and achieving your goals.

Seek Social Support:

Share your goals with friends or family who can provide encouragement and hold you accountable. Having a support system can make it easier to stick to your self-control efforts.

Track and Monitor Progress:

Keep a record of your successes and setbacks. This tracking helps you identify patterns, adjust your strategies, and stay motivated by seeing your progress.

Practice Self-Compassion:

Be kind and forgiving to yourself when you slip up. Self-compassion reduces the negative emotions associated with failures, making it easier to get back on track.

Consistency is Key:

Consistently practice self-control and discipline. Over time, it becomes a habit that is easier to maintain.

Learn from Setbacks:

Instead of viewing setbacks as failures, see them as opportunities to learn and grow. Analyze what went wrong and adjust your strategies accordingly.

Applied psychology teaches us that self-control is a skill that can be developed and strengthened over time. By applying these principles and techniques, you can enhance your self-control, which in turn will empower you to achieve virtually anything you set your mind to. Remember that self-control is a valuable asset in both personal and professional endeavors, and it's worth the effort to cultivate it.

Build Habits

Habits are automated behaviors that require less willpower to execute. Create positive habits that support your goals. Start small, and gradually increase the complexity of these habits as they become ingrained in your routine.

Building habits is a crucial aspect of achieving your goals and can be effectively approached using principles from applied psychology. Here's a detailed explanation of how to build habits that will help you accomplish anything you want:

Break It Down:

Divide your goal into smaller, manageable steps or sub-goals. This makes it less overwhelming and easier to work on consistently.

Identify Existing Habits:

Take stock of your current habits, both positive and negative, that may impact your goal. Understanding your existing routines will help you incorporate new habits effectively.

Start Small:

Begin with a small and achievable habit related to your goal. Starting small makes it easier to build momentum and prevents burnout or frustration.

Set a Trigger:

Identify a specific trigger or cue that will remind you to perform the habit. It could be a time of day, a location, or an action you already do consistently.

Create a Routine:

Develop a clear routine or action plan for your habit. Make it as simple and straightforward as possible to reduce resistance.

Use Positive Reinforcement:

Reward yourself each time you successfully complete the habit. Positive reinforcement strengthens the neural pathways associated with the habit, making it more likely to stick.

Practice Consistency:

Consistency is key to habit formation. Commit to performing the habit at the designated trigger and time consistently, ideally daily.

Track Your Progress:

Keep a record of your habit-building journey. This can be as simple as marking an X on a calendar or using habit-tracking apps. Tracking helps you stay accountable.

Visualize Success:

Visualization techniques can be powerful. Picture yourself successfully performing the habit and achieving your goal. This can boost motivation and commitment.

Implement Accountability:

Share your habit-building journey with a friend, family member, or mentor who can hold you accountable. Regular check-ins can provide encouragement and motivation.

Use Implementation Intentions:

Formulate clear "if-then" statements related to your habit. For example, "If it's 6 AM, then I will go for a run." This mental planning can help you respond to triggers consistently.

Learn from Setbacks:

Expect occasional setbacks and view them as opportunities for learning and growth. Analyze what went wrong and adjust your strategy accordingly.

Gradually Increase Complexity:

Once the initial habit is firmly established, gradually increase its complexity or intensity to align with your ultimate goal.

Be Patient:

Habits take time to solidify. Be patient and realistic about the time it will take to achieve your goal through habit-building.

Avoid Overloading:

Don't try to build too many habits at once. Focus on one or a few key habits related to your primary goal to avoid overwhelm.

Review and Adjust:

Periodically review your habits and their effectiveness in helping you achieve your goal. Be willing to adjust your approach based on your experiences and results.

Habit-building based on applied psychology principles leverages our understanding of behavior change and motivation. By following these steps and being persistent, you can establish habits that support your goals and increase your chances of achieving anything you set your mind to. Remember that building habits is a process, and with dedication and consistency, you can make remarkable progress over time.

If you're struggling to build a habit or encounter psychological barriers, consider seeking help from a therapist or coach who specializes in behavior change.

Embrace Discomfort

Understand that growth often occurs outside your comfort zone. Accept discomfort as a natural part of the journey towards your goals. Challenge yourself to step into uncomfortable situations willingly.

Embracing discomfort is a crucial aspect of achieving your goals and personal growth, drawing from applied psychology principles. Here's a detailed explanation of how to do this effectively:

Understand the Nature of Discomfort:

Recognize that discomfort is a natural response to situations that challenge your comfort zone. It often signifies growth opportunities. Applied psychology tells us that humans tend to seek comfort, but lasting personal development requires pushing beyond these boundaries.

Set Clear and Compelling Goals:

Clearly state what you hope to accomplish. Make sure your objectives are both motivating and personally meaningful. You'll be able to bear discomfort if you have a compelling "why" for your goals.

Re-frame Your Perspective:

Change how you view discomfort. Instead of seeing it as something to avoid, think of it as a sign of progress. Recognize that discomfort is a necessary part of the path to success and growth.

Break Down Goals into Smaller Steps:

Divide your grand goals into manageable, lesser tasks. This approach lessens the paralyzing agony that comes from taking on a significant endeavor.

Gradual Exposure:

In applied psychology, gradual exposure therapy is widely used to help patients get over their phobias or worries. Apply a similar principle to discomfort by progressively exposing yourself to it. Start with simpler tasks and work your way up to more challenging ones.

Visualization and Mental Rehearsal:

Use visualization techniques to psychologically prepare for discomfort. Imagine being able to handle difficult situations with ease. This can help you feel more confident and less anxious.

Practice Mindfulness:

You can learn to examine your thoughts and feelings without passing judgment through meditation and other mindfulness exercises like these, which will help you respond to discomfort more objectively.

Seek Support and Accountability:

It can be simpler to control your discomfort if you have someone to share it with. Tell a friend, mentor, or coach you can rely on about your objectives so they can support you and hold you accountable.

Embrace a Growth Mindset:

Accept a growth mindset, which holds that effort and education can improve one's abilities and intelligence. This perspective of view enables you to regard discomfort as an opportunity for growth rather than a barrier.

Celebrate Small Wins:

Whatever your accomplishments may seem to be, acknowledge and appreciate them. These events serve as a source of inspiration for you to keep accepting discomfort.

Monitor Your Progress:

Maintain a regular evaluation of your progress. With the help of this tracking, you can stay on course and adjust your strategy as needed.

Embrace a Growth-Oriented Environment:

Spend time with people who share your ideals and who encourage your own growth. Your environment has a big impact on your ability to accept hardship and reach your goals.

Stay Persistent:

Recognize that discomfort is a constant companion on the path to success. By tolerating difficulties and discomfort on a regular basis, you can eventually achieve remarkable results.

By using these psychological concepts to your daily life, you can successfully embrace discomfort as a tool to achieve anything you desire. Remember that discomfort is not the adversary, but rather an essential instrument for achievement and growth on the personal level.

CHAPTER THREE

Develop Resilience

The capacity to recover from failures and setbacks is resilience. Recognize that there will be challenges along the way. Consider these difficulties as chances to improve yourself rather than as a reason to give up.

A key component of accomplishing your goals and overcoming challenges is building resilience. In the context of applied psychology, resilience is the capacity to overcome adversity, adjust to change, and uphold well-being despite hardships. Here's a thorough description of how to build resilience so you can accomplish everything you set your mind to:

Understand Resilience:

Start by comprehending what resilience is. Instead of trying to escape problems, one should learn how to deal with them and recover from them. Developing a resilient mentality and set of abilities will help you face challenges head-on and come out stronger.

Cultivate a Growth Mindset:

Adopt a growth mindset, which is the idea that one can improve one's skills and intelligence by working hard and learning new things. This way of thinking enables you to see obstacles as chances for development rather than as limitations on your potential.

Develop Self-Awareness:

Endurance depends heavily on self-awareness. Recognize your feelings, your assets, and your flaws. Recognize your regular coping mechanisms under pressure and adversity. This knowledge enables you to make wise decisions under trying circumstances.

Build Strong Relationships:

Resilience is significantly influenced by social support. Develop enduring, uplifting bonds with your friends, family, and role models. During trying times, these relationships offer crucial viewpoints, encouragement, and emotional support.

Enhance Problem-Solving Skills:

Finding beneficial solutions to issues is a key component of resilience. By breaking down problems into smaller, more manageable steps and coming up with solutions, you can improve your problem-solving abilities. Request input and gain knowledge from your experiences.

Foster Emotional Regulation:

Effective emotion management requires practice. You can learn to control your emotional reactions to stress and adversity by practicing methods like mindfulness meditation, deep breathing exercises, and journaling.

Practice Adaptability:

There are many unforeseen changes in life. Be open to new experiences and flexible with your goals to practice adaptability. Resilience is largely characterized by flexibility.

Develop Coping Strategies:

Find healthy coping mechanisms that are effective for you. Exercise, creative outlets, getting professional assistance when necessary, and practicing relaxation techniques are a few examples. Create a toolkit of coping techniques.

Cultivate Optimism:

Positivity should become your way of life. In trying circumstances, optimism keeps you motivated and hopeful. Concentrate on your assets, previous achievements, and the likelihood of success.

Learn from Failure:

It's inevitable to fail in life. Take it as a learning opportunity rather than a setback. Examine what went wrong, make necessary changes to your strategy, and use what you learned to guide future work.

Practice Resilience Daily:

Over time, resilience is a skill that may be acquired. By purposefully seeking out challenges, putting up with discomfort, and overcoming adversity, you can put it into practice every day.

Build a Support Network:

Create a network of friends, family, or support organizations. Making connections with people who have encountered like difficulties can be extremely insightful and uplifting.

Self-Care:

Make self-care routines like getting adequate sleep, eating healthily, and exercising frequently a priority. Emotional resilience is significantly influenced by physical health.

Reflect and Re-frame:

Think back on your experiences often, especially when things are difficult. Transform negative thoughts into ones that are more uplifting and beneficial. Defeat mental distortions that may weaken your resilience.

Patience and Persistence:

Resilience training is an ongoing practice. Be kind to yourself as you constantly seek to develop greater resilience over time.

Don't be reluctant to seek assistance from a therapist or counselor if you are struggling to develop resilience on your own or are dealing with overwhelming problems. They are able to offer direction, advice, and support.

You can develop the inner fortitude and adaptability required to accomplish your objectives and flourish in the face of adversity by using these resilience-building techniques from the field of applied psychology. Resilience is not just recovering from setbacks but also developing stronger and more seasoned as a result of them.

Use Rewards and Punishments

Use a system of rewards and penalties to help people learn to be more self-disciplined. Give yourself prizes when you reach goals and withhold them when you don't follow through with your strategy. This offers prompt encouragement and feedback.

A key idea in applied psychology is the appropriate use of rewards and penalties to help you accomplish your goals. This strategy makes use of behavior modification principles to inspire self-motivation for desired results. Here's a thorough breakdown of how to utilize incentives and penalties to get anything you want:

Understand the Basics:

External cues like rewards and penalties have an impact on behavior. While punishments lower the likelihood of a behavior being repeated, rewards boost it. This is referred to as operant conditioning, a behaviorist psychology idea created by B.F. Skinner.

Define Clear Goals:

Start by establishing definite, defined goals for yourself. Make sure your objectives can be attained within a practical time limit and are realistic.

Break Goals into Smaller Tasks:

Break down your most ambitious objectives into more doable chores. This makes it simpler to monitor progress and assign incentives and penalties to particular behaviors.

Identify Appropriate Rewards:

Rewards should have personal value for you and serve as motivation. Treats, gifts, and a night out are just a few examples of tangible rewards. Intangible rewards include praise, self-affirmation, and more time.

Determine Punishments:

On the other side, you ought to try to stay away from punishments. They shouldn't be unduly severe or harmful, but they should have a negative effect if you don't achieve your objectives. This could involve delaying a beloved activity, allocating more time for work, or paying a minor fine.

Set Milestones:

Set up clear checkpoints on the way to your objective. Each achievement stands for a moment at which you can evaluate your development and impose incentives or penalties.

Monitor and Track Progress:

Keep track of your efforts and advancement. You can assess the success of your rewards and punishments by monitoring your behaviors and outcomes.

Apply Immediate and Consistent Consequences:

Rewards and penalties must precisely coincide with the behavior in order to be successful. Immediate feedback makes it easier to make a clear relationship between an activity and its results. To reinforce the desired behavior, use rewards and penalties consistently.

Make Rewards and Punishments Proportional:

The size of the prize or punishment should correspond to how important the action was. Smaller accomplishments could call for smaller awards, whilst bigger accomplishments might call for bigger prizes.

Use Positive Reinforcement:

In order to encourage desired behaviors, you might give yourself rewards. For instance, if your objective is to exercise frequently, treat yourself to a soothing bath or a tasty treat after a productive workout.

Implement Negative Reinforcement Sparingly:

When a behavior is being reinforced negatively, an unpleasant stimulus is removed. While in some circumstances this may be useful, it is generally preferable to concentrate on positive reinforcement in order to establish a more uplifting and long-lasting motivation cycle.

Be Careful with Punishments:

If punishments are too harsh or repeated, they may be demotivating. They should act as a deterrent, but not as a catalyst for excessive negativity or feelings of helplessness. Make sure they are fair and reasonable before using them.

Adjust as Needed:

As you move closer to your goals, be flexible and open to change your reward and punishment scheme. If you discover that some incentives aren't motivating you as intended, experiment with others until you find the one that does.

Reflect and Adapt:

Review your progress and the efficiency of your reward and punishment approach on a regular basis. To maintain your motivation high and your goals reachable, adjust it as necessary.

Seek External Accountability:

Tell a friend, relative, or mentor about your objectives and your rewards and punishments so they can help hold you accountable and give you more drive.

You can develop a strong motivational system to assist you in achieving your goals by using the principles of operant conditioning and behavior modification through rewards and punishments. This strategy makes use of the psychology of reward and motivation to encourage positive behavior change and raise your chances of success in a variety of areas of your life.

Seek Social Support

Share your objectives with close relatives and friends or a mentor who can help you stay on track. Spend time with people who will inspire and support you on your journey.

An effective method for attaining your goals that is grounded in applied psychology is asking for social support. Humans are naturally social creatures, thus making use of others' encouragement can greatly improve your motivation, responsibility, and chances of success. Here is a thorough discussion of the best way to ask for social support:

Identify Your Support Network:

Finding the people in your life who can offer assistance should be your first step. This can include members of your family, friends, mentors, coworkers, or a support group for people pursuing similar goals.

Share Your Goals:

Tell your network of supporters your objectives in a direct manner. Clearly state what you hope to accomplish and why it matters to you. In your conversation, be enthusiastic and specific.

Choose the Right People:

Think about the qualifications and experience of the people you share your objectives with. Look for individuals that have the necessary expertise, experience, or a stake in your success. Be in the company of supportive and motivating people.

Seek Accountability Partners:

Accountability partners are those who frequently check in on your progress to help keep you on track. Select a trustworthy person who will hold you accountable without passing judgment.

Set Expectations:

Determine each member of your support network's function in detail. Tell them how they can assist you, whether it is by giving you advice, listening to you, encouraging you, or taking part in activities that are linked to your objective.

Leverage Online Communities:

You can meet people who share your interests and are working toward the same objectives through online communities, forums, and social media groups. These groups provide a forum for exchanging knowledge and soliciting advice from a larger network.

Join a Mastermind Group:

Individuals that participate in mastermind groups gather frequently to talk about their objectives, difficulties, and advancement. They offer a disciplined setting for exchanging ideas, getting criticism, and holding one another accountable.

Be Selective About Feedback:

Not all criticism has the same value. Ask for helpful criticism from people who are knowledgeable about your field. Instead of viewing feedback as criticism, think of it as a way to get better.

Express Gratitude:

Support from a professional may be required in some circumstances. This can entail working with a coach, therapist, or consultant with expertise in the region crucial to achieving your objective.

Communicate Progress and Challenges:

Inform your network of supporters frequently about your achievements and difficulties. Share both your achievements and your failures so that they can offer you individualized support and encouragement.

Manage Expectations:

Be reasonable in your expectations of your support system. Recognize that they have their own obligations and restrictions. Don't just rely on other people to motivate you; you also need to motivate yourself.

Respect Boundaries:

Respect your support network's restrictions and bounds. Keep in mind that not everyone can be available at all times.

Reciprocate Support:

Be prepared to lend a helping hand when your friends or coworkers do as well. Developing a mutually beneficial relationship expands your network and fosters a sense of community.

Seek Professional Support:

Support from a professional may be required in some circumstances. This can entail working with a coach, therapist, or consultant with expertise in the region crucial to achieving your objective.

Regularly Evaluate Your Network:

Evaluate your support system's effectiveness on a regular basis. Establish whether some people or organizations are more beneficial than others, and then modify your network accordingly.

Stay Open to Diverse Perspectives:

Accept different perspectives and backgrounds from your network of friends. New ideas and creative solutions might result from various viewpoints.

Maintain a Positive Attitude:

Enthusiasm and optimism spread easily. When asking for help, keep a positive outlook because this will inspire others to support your cause.

Based on these applied psychology principles, you can actively seek out social support to build a network of people who inspire and encourage you to achieve your objectives. Keep in mind that important aspects of your path to success include your capacity to maintain healthy relationships and the caliber of your support network.

Monitor Progress

Maintain a regular progress log and revise your strategy as necessary. This assists you in staying on track and making the required adjustments.

According to the theories of applied psychology, tracking progress is an essential component of reaching any objective. You can stay on course, make wise modifications, and keep your enthusiasm up with its assistance. Here's a thorough breakdown on how to efficiently keep track of your development:

Define Clear Metrics:

To begin, identify precise metrics or indications that you will use to track your progress toward your objective. These indicators ought to be measurable and pertinent to your goal. For instance, if your objective is to lose weight, measurements can include weight loss, circumference reduction, or body fat percentage.

Set Milestones and Deadlines:

Divide your long-term objective into more manageable, time-bound objectives. Your progress is tracked by these milestones, which can help your objective seem less daunting. Every accomplishment should be a big step toward your ultimate goal.

Use a Journal or Tracking System:

Regularly document your progress in a notebook, online spreadsheet, or monitoring application. This enables you to organize and record your efforts, setbacks, and successes. Make entries on a regular basis; daily, weekly, or monthly.

Measure Consistently:

Make sure you utilize the established metrics to continuously track your progress. For reliable tracking, measurement consistency is crucial. Avoid taking measurements too often (which can inspire despondency) or infrequently (which can cause you to lose sight of your objective).

Compare Results to Baseline:

Compare your most recent findings to your initial measurement baselines. This gives you a clear picture of your development and enables you to appropriately assess it.

Adjust Your Plan as Needed:

Review your progress data frequently to determine if you're on schedule to achieve your milestones and long-term objective. Be prepared to modify your plan if you're running behind schedule or running into unanticipated difficulties. The secret to long-term success is adaptability.

Analyze Setbacks Objectively:

When you face challenges or setbacks, approach them objectively and with a growth perspective. Examine what went wrong, the reasons it occurred, and the lessons you may draw from it. You can prevent recurring errors and make the necessary modifications with the aid of this analysis.

Stay Accountable:

With a supportive friend, mentor, or accountability partner, discuss your progress and goals. Having someone hold you accountable can help with motivation and provide you an outside view of your development

.

Use Visualization Techniques:

Visualization is a potent tool for tracking development. Think on yourself accomplishing your objectives, which can increase motivation and self-assurance.

Monitor Emotional Well-being:

The entire trip, pay attention to your emotional health. The psychological component of achieving goals is essential. Address any feelings of discouragement or lack of motivation as soon as you notice them. Self-compassion and mindfulness exercises can be helpful.

Reflect and Adjust:

Take time from time to time to consider your overall progress and the efficacy of your initiatives. To make sure you're always moving in the right path, modify your plan and goals based on your reflections.

Seek Feedback:

Don't hesitate to seek feedback from others who have expertise or experience in your area of pursuit. Constructive feedback can provide valuable insights for improvement.

Stay Committed:

Last but not least, stay committed to your objectives and the monitoring procedure. For long-term effectiveness, consistency in monitoring and responding to changes is essential.

You may maintain your concentration, motivation, and accountability by tracking your progress using applied psychology principles. You may use it to make data-driven decisions, gain knowledge from your mistakes, and eventually accomplish your goals. Keep in mind that reaching important goals frequently needs ongoing self-evaluation and change to make sure you're moving in the right way.

CHAPTER FOUR

Visualize Success

To visualize yourself attaining your goals, use visualization techniques. Your motivation and confidence can both be increased by this mental practice.

By utilizing the power of your imagination and belief systems, the powerful approach of visualizing success can assist you in reaching your goals. Here is a thorough description of how to successfully picture achievement to fulfill any desire:

Define Your Goal:

Start by outlining your objective in detail. Be as specific as you can when describing your goals. Your aim will be easier to visualize if it is more specific.

Find a Quiet and Comfortable Space:

Find a peaceful, comfortable location where you won't be bothered so that you can think successfully. Your mental focus will improve as a result.

Relax and Breathe:

Start by taking a few slow, deep breaths. your body and mind to calmness. The most effective condition for visualization is one of calm.

Create a Mental Image:

Close your eyes and visualize yourself accomplishing your goal in great detail. Think of it as if it were currently occurring. To create a realistic and vivid image, use all of your senses.
Do you see anything? Visualize the environment, the people, and the specifics.
Do you hear anything? Include any sounds that are connected to your success.
How are you feeling? Feel the feelings and sensations that come with your success.
What can you taste and smell? Include any flavors or scents, as appropriate, in your visualization.

Engage Your Emotions:

Immerse yourself in the satisfying feelings connected to your success as you picture. Experience the happiness, fulfillment, pride, and self-assurance that come with completing your goal.

Make it Personal:

Think of yourself as the protagonist of your own success tale. The vision is more effective and inspiring because of this individual connection.

Be Realistic:

While having ambitious goals is important, keep your imagination grounded in reality. Set controllable, attainable goals in your mind's eye.

Use Affirmations:

Include uplifting statements in your visualization. Repeat to yourself encouraging phrases about your success. For instance, "I can do this," "I'm committed to doing this," etc.

Visualize the Process:

Don't only concentrate on the outcome. Consider the actions you must take to get there. Imagine yourself putting in a lot of effort, getting through obstacles, and progressing.

Practice Regularly:

Key is consistency. Establish a daily visualization routine, ideally in the morning or right before bed. Your confidence in your capacity to accomplish your goal is strengthened by repetition.

Use Visualization as Motivation:

In times of difficulty or self-doubt, go back to your visualization. Make use of it as inspiration and a reminder of why you are pursuing your objective.

Monitor and Adjust:

Update your visualization as you move closer to your objective to reflect your changing circumstances and goals. To keep your mental image motivating and current, adjust it.

Combine Visualization with Action:

Your goals won't materialize in a magical way just by using visualization. Inspire action with your visuals. Take actionable measures in the direction of your objective while remaining confident in your success.

Stay Patient and Persistent:

Recognize that reaching important goals requires time and effort. You can use visualization as a technique to help you remain patient and persistent during your journey.

According to applied psychology, visualization increases your likelihood of succeeding by coordinating your subconscious goals with your cognitive ones. You can improve your self-confidence, motivation, and attention by regularly engaging in visualization exercises, which will ultimately increase your chances of succeeding in anything you set out to do.

Stay Consistent

The secret to developing self-discipline is consistency. Even on the days when you lack motivation, follow your plan. Discipline develops into a habit over time.

Achieving your goals requires constancy in your efforts, and applied psychology has some advice on how to do that. Here is a thorough description of how to continue working toward your goals:

Break Goals into Smaller Steps:

Break up your objectives into more doable, smaller steps or milestones. Smaller chores are easier to complete and give you a feeling of achievement, which might inspire you to continue.

Create a Concrete Plan:

Create a thorough plan that describes the precise steps you must take to accomplish your objectives. A road-map makes it simpler to stay on course and lowers the likelihood of wandering off course.

Prioritize Tasks:

Organize your duties according to their urgency and importance. By doing so, you may stay on task and avoid procrastination.

Develop Positive Habits:

Consistency is powerfully aided by habits. Work on implementing the habits that will help you achieve your goals into your regular activities. Start modest and progressively increase your efforts.

Use Behavioral Triggers:

Connect your desired behaviors to current routines or cues. For instance, immediately after brushing your teeth in the morning, if you want to engage in regular activity. This establishes a habit loop that strengthens reliability.

Set a Schedule:

Create a consistent schedule for achieving your goals. Following a routine is a good way to be consistent. Give your goal-related duties a specific amount of time each day or each week.

Visualize Success:

To visualize your success, use visualization techniques. Imagining the fruit of your labors might help you stay motivated and consistent.

Monitor Progress:

Maintain a regular progress log. You can do this by keeping a notebook, utilizing goal-tracking applications, or any other strategy that suits your needs. You can stay responsible and change course when necessary by monitoring.

Seek Accountability:

Tell a mentor, family member, or close friend about your objectives so they can help hold you accountable. Consistency can be improved by giving someone else regular updates or check-ins.

Embrace Setbacks:

Recognize that challenges and setbacks are a necessary part of the process. Utilize them as teaching opportunities rather than allowing them to hinder your growth. Consider what went wrong and modify your approach.

Practice Self-Compassion:

When you face obstacles or experience setbacks, be kind and understanding with yourself. Self-criticism should be avoided as it might undermine drive and consistency.

Stay Focused on the Why:

Remind yourself often of the initial motivation behind your goal-setting. Your dedication may be rekindled by getting in touch with your fundamental motives.

Find Intrinsic Motivation:

Remind yourself often of the initial motivation behind your goal-setting. Your dedication may be rekindled by getting in touch with your fundamental motives.

Use Positive Self-Talk:

Pay attention to your inner dialogue and replace unfavorable or self-defeating thoughts with supportive ones. Your constancy may be enhanced through self-encouragement.

Create a Supportive Environment:

Surround yourself with people, things, and a setting that will help you achieve your objectives. Reduce interruptions and make an environment that supports your work.

Review and Adjust:

Review your objectives, performance, and tactics frequently. To keep on track and maintain consistency, be prepared to modify your plan as necessary.

Applied psychology reminds us that consistency is about setting up the ideal environment and mentality for success, not just about willpower. You can greatly enhance your capacity to maintain consistency and accomplish your goals by implementing these tactics into your life and comprehending the psychological principles that behind them.

Practice Self-Compassion

When you have setbacks, be kind to yourself. Self-compassion lessens the unpleasant feelings brought on by failure and makes it easier for you to recover.

In order to achieve your goals, practicing self-compassion is essential since it aids in keeping a good outlook, overcoming obstacles, and remaining motivated. Applied psychology offers suggestions on how to develop self-compassion so that you can attain your goals:

Understand Self-Compassion:

Learn the definition of self-compassion first. When you have challenges or disappointments, it entails treating oneself with the same compassion, consideration, and understanding that you would extend to a friend. It involves accepting your humanity and flaws.

Practice Self-Awareness:

Learn to notice when you're being harsh or critical of yourself by developing self-awareness. Be aware of your inner conversation for any critical or negative thoughts. Making meaningful changes begins with raising awareness.

Challenge Negative Self-Talk:

Challenge your thoughts when you notice yourself using critical or negative self-talk. Consider whether you would address a friend in a comparable scenario with the same words. Substitute self-compassionate phrases for self-critical ones.

Develop Self-Kindness:

Be kind to yourself and gentle with yourself. Offer yourself words of support and encouragement rather than criticizing your errors or failings. Saying things like "I'll do better next time" or "It's okay; everyone makes mistakes" will help you to be kind to yourself.

Embrace Imperfection:

Recognize that the idea of perfection is unattainable. Accept your flaws and understand that making mistakes is a necessary part of learning. Your flaws are what make you human; they do not determine your value.

Practice Mindfulness:

Being in the moment without passing judgment is a component of mindfulness. Practice mindfulness to examine your thoughts and feelings without giving them a bad name. You can prevent getting sucked into self-critical thinking by doing this.

Cultivate Self-Compassionate Self-Talk:

Make a list of affirmations or statements that encourage self-compassion. These words can be used to combat self-criticism and strengthen self-compassion. Examples include "I am doing my best, and that is enough," or "I am worthy of love and acceptance."

Learn from Setbacks:

Consider setbacks as chances for growth and learning rather than failures. Consider what went wrong, what you can do better, and how you can proceed in the future. This positive outlook aids in your ability to recover more quickly.

Develop a Self-Compassion Routine:

Adopt self-compassion as a daily practice. Make time for self-analysis, self-compassion training, or mindfulness practices. Your self-compassion muscle will get stronger when you are consistent.

Seek Support and Feedback:

Speak with your friends, relatives, or a therapist who can offer you emotional support and helpful criticism. Sharing your struggles with others can help you feel less alone and less critical of yourself.

Avoid Self-Pity:

Be careful not to lapse into self-pity when engaging in the practice of self-compassion. Acknowledging your suffering without exaggerating it is a key component of self-compassion. A balanced viewpoint that promotes growth in oneself.

Set Realistic Expectations:

Stay away from having unrealistic or too high expectations for oneself. Be honest with yourself about what you can accomplish in a certain amount of time. Having realistic expectations lessens the chance of self-criticism.

Remember Your Why:

Remind yourself of the primary motivation behind your pursuit of your objectives. Get in touch with your inner drive and the more profound motivations driving your objectives. This can support your commitment and compassion for yourself when things get tough.

Practice Patience:

Recognize that achieving goals and growing personally takes time. As you strive toward your goals, be patient with yourself. You can tolerate setbacks and keep a long-term perspective when you have self-compassion.

You can cultivate a nurturing and encouraging internal environment that promotes resilience and perseverance by engaging in self-compassion practices. This optimistic outlook, which is grounded on applied psychology, can enable you to overcome challenges, recover from setbacks, and eventually accomplish your goals in life while upholding a good sense of self-worth and well-being.

Review and Reflect

Review your progress frequently and consider what's working and what isn't. Adapt your plans and objectives as necessary.

Reviewing and reflecting are crucial steps in achieving goals and growing personally because they let you gauge your success, take lessons from past mistakes, and modify your strategy as necessary. Achieving your goals can be done more effectively by reviewing and reflecting, according to the application of psychology. Here is a thorough description of this procedure:

Set Aside Dedicated Time:

Plan frequent, devoted time for thought and evaluation. Depending on the nature and size of your goals, this could be done daily, weekly, or monthly. To develop this as a habit, one must be consistent.

Create a Reflective Environment:

Locate a peaceful, relaxing area where you may concentrate without being disturbed. To write down your reflections, think about utilizing a notebook or a digital note-taking app.

Define Clear Objectives:

Establish the goal of your review and reflection session before you start. Are you examining previous decisions, monitoring the status of a certain objective, or looking for opportunities for personal development?

Gather Data and Information:

Gather pertinent facts and data about your objectives and past experiences. This could be memos, papers, reviews, or stats on performance.

Ask the Right Questions:

Asking yourself insightful questions will help you think more deeply and become more self-aware. Here are a few instances:
- What strides have I made toward achieving my objectives since my last assessment?
- What did and didn't work well?
- What obstacles did I face, and how did I overcome them?
- What lessons have I taken away from my experiences?
- Do my actions or results have any patterns or trends?
- How can I adjust my strategy going forward?
- Are my priorities and values still in line with my goals?

Analyze and Evaluate:

Use the data you've obtained to analyze and impartially assess your performance. Take into account both quantitative and qualitative facts, as well as your feelings regarding the events you have had.

Embrace Mistakes and Failures:

Don't be afraid to analyze your shortcomings or mistakes. They provide worthwhile opportunities for education. Concentrate on what you can learn from them and how you can get better rather than focusing on them.

Identify Patterns and Trends:

Analyze your actions, choices, or results for any recurring patterns or trends. You can make better decisions in the future by recognizing these trends.

Set New Goals and Adjust Plans:

Set new goals or revise your present ones in light of your analysis and evaluation. Make sure your objectives continue to reflect your values and aspirations.

Prioritize Actions:

Based on your reflections, compile a list of doable actions and solutions. To make these acts more feasible, divide them into smaller, more manageable tasks.

Monitor Progress:

Follow your development toward your newly established objectives. Make sure your actions are taking you in the right direction at all times.

Seek Feedback:

Ask for input from mentors, peers, or other reliable people who can offer an objective assessment of your objectives and development, if appropriate.

Practice Gratitude:

Spend a time being thankful for the chances you have and the advancements you have made. Gratitude can encourage a positive outlook and enhance general well-being.

Repeat the Process:

Regularly incorporate reflection and evaluation into your habit. Each session builds on the one before it, assisting you in improving your methods and achieving your objectives more successfully.

Stay Patient and Flexible:

Recognize that achieving goals and growing personally are iterative processes. Be kind to yourself, flexible, and willing to change as necessary.

Self-awareness, learning from experiences, and changing to better performance are all stressed in applied psychology. You may use these principles to accomplish anything you want while continuously improving and becoming the best version of yourself by reviewing and reflecting on your objectives and activities on a frequent basis.

Patience and Persistence

Recognize that reaching important goals requires time. Even when progress seems to be slow, be persistent. Continue forward and have faith in the process.

Long-term success in any activity requires the traits of patience and persistence, both of which are firmly anchored in rules of applied psychology. How to develop and preserve these abilities is explained in detail below:

Break Down Goals into Smaller Steps:

Create smaller, more doable tasks or milestones for each of your goals. Utilizing this strategy reduces feelings of overload and enables you to concentrate on one step at a time. Having these minor successes might increase your patience and motivation.

Develop Intrinsic Motivation:

Patience and perseverance are greatly aided by intrinsic motivation, which is the desire to pursue objectives for their own sake rather than for the sake of receiving outside benefits. Consider the reasons that your goals mean something to you personally and connect with the inner desire that drives them.

Cultivate Self-Compassion:

When you have setbacks or difficulties, be nice and compassionate to yourself. Reduced negative emotions brought on by failures make it simpler to move on and maintain patience.

Practice Self-Control:

Self-control is the capacity to restrain impulses and maintain attention on long-term goals. Develop the ability to choose consciously and in ways that support your objectives. Self-control can be improved via methods like mindfulness.

Develop Resilience:

Be prepared for challenges and setbacks on your road. Consider them opportunities to learn and develop rather than failures. Resilience is the capacity to overcome challenges and emerge stronger.

Use Visualization Techniques:

Regularly envision your success. Clearly picture yourself attaining your objectives. This mental practice can increase your patience and self-assurance, enabling you to stick with your course of action.

Build a Support System:

Be in the company of people who will inspire you when things get tough and who will support your aspirations. Share your successes and setbacks with them since having someone hold you accountable may keep you motivated.

Monitor Progress and Adjust:

Maintain a progress log and revisit your objectives and plan of action frequently. Be prepared to change your strategy if you discover something isn't working. The ability to adapt is essential for long-term success.

Embrace the Journey:

Recognize that accomplishing your goals requires a process as crucial as the final product. Accept the voyage, and take pleasure in the advancements you make along the route.

Cultivate Patience through Mindfulness:

By teaching you to stay present and composed in the face of difficulties, mindfulness techniques like meditation can aid in the development of patience. Additionally, these methods lessen impulsivity.

Focus on the Big Picture:

Remember your long-term goals. Remind yourself of the benefits and rewards that coming to fruition will bring. You can preserve your tenacity and patience by adopting this viewpoint.

Celebrate Small Wins:

Recognize and appreciate your accomplishments, regardless of how minor they may seem. These occasions might encourage you and strengthen your perseverance.

Learn from Failures:

Consider failures as useful teaching opportunities rather than as defeats. Examine what went wrong, then apply what you learned to modify your tactics and approach.

Cultivate Optimism:

Your patience and resilience may both increase with an optimistic outlook. Maintain an optimistic outlook and have faith in your capacity to overcome obstacles.

Applying these theories from applied psychology will help you cultivate the perseverance and patience necessary to accomplish almost anything you set your mind to. Always keep in mind that these are abilities that can be developed and improved through time, ultimately resulting in more success and fulfillment in your life.